D1147946

GILES

An Hachette UK Company
www.hachette.co.uk

First published in Great Britain in 2017 by Hamlyn,
a division of Octopus Publishing Group Ltd, Carmelite House,
50 Victoria Embankment, London EC4Y 0DZ
www.octopusbooks.co.uk

Cartoons
British Cartoon Archive

Cartoons supplied by British Cartoon Archive
Cartoons compiled by John Field

ISBN 978 0 60062 956 6

A CIP catalogue record for this book is available from the British Library.

Printed and bound in China

10 9 8 7 6 5 4 3 2 1

The Collection 2018

compiled by John Field
foreword by Bill Turnbull

EXPRESS NEWSPAPERS
hamlyn

Contents

Foreword

Bill Turnbull

Leafing through a Giles collection is like stepping back in time. Or rather, enjoying a gentle stroll through the landscape of the past in the company of an old but very humorous friend – warm memories of days gone by.

I first came across this great artist more than 50 years ago, back when the *Daily Express* was still a broadsheet. There was just one copy of each newspaper to share among the boarders at what I remember as a grim and rather penal prep school. Giles was our favourite cartoonist and we jostled to get to the *Express* to see what he had to say. No fierce political caricatures for him, just a sideways look at events from the viewpoint of the common man, woman, or Grandma. Jokes that an eight-year-old could understand, that would often have you nodding in agreement.

Much of what Giles drew then is social history now. Strikes and industrial disputes seemed as regular as rain. A British "staycation" wasn't an amusing novelty, it was all that people could afford. Before the days of cheap flights, totalitarian boarding houses and "ram-packed" (to coin a phrase) beaches were a fact of holiday life for most Brits.

And of course there was the weather. Giles's holidays were almost invariably afflicted by raging tempest and flood, and so were ours. One of my earliest memories is of bawling on a Cornish beach being sheltered by my mother, as the sand whipped viciously around us, and that was before the inevitable downpours. Holidays were like that then and Giles captured them beautifully.

I have two things in common with him: I now live not far from where he resided in the beautiful county of Suffolk and we both went on caravan holidays (although I think Giles must have enjoyed his much more than I did ours). Turnbull family tours of Scotland, Cornwall, France and beyond were punctuated by rows, tears, getting lost, mechanical breakdowns, bad meals and stomach upsets, perfumed by the delicate fragrance of propane gas, chemical loos and the cheroots my Dad insisted on smoking in the car – surely all ingredients for a classic Giles cartoon.

Christmas, another theme of this volume, doesn't get off lightly either. Not for Giles a cosy idealized season of peace and goodwill. His vision is one of bad-tempered shop assistants, mayhem and merriment at office parties, and domestic discord fuelled by alcoholic overindulgence. Just about right, then.

What makes Giles special is not just his wry view of life. Each of his pictures is more than a mere cartoon; it's a tableau. There is so much more detail to them than just the central joke: a snot-nosed kid lurking round a corner, the boot-faced aunt on the sofa, the parrot at the top of the Christmas tree. Perhaps it's the comforting certainty of history, but looking back now, it seems like a simpler, calmer world. No computers, no internet, no mobile phones, let alone "smart" ones. What would Giles have made of all that? And more importantly, what would Grandma?

So I hope you enjoy this gentle look back at the past. If you were there at the time, long-forgotten incidents may pop back into your memory. And if you weren't, you'll be interested to see how much life has moved on, for better or worse. For instance: one cartoon covering a fuel shortage from December 1974 (one of several in those years), has an angry motorist fulminating at a filling station: "Don't you Merry Christmas me at 73p a gallon!"

That's 16p a litre. Happy days.

Introduction: Holidays

The theme of this year's collection is the three main British holiday periods – Summer, Christmas and Easter. Nowadays foreign travel has become the norm but for much of Giles's cartooning career this was not the case. During the earlier period of his work people generally took holidays in this country and therefore many of his summer holiday cartoons refer to the British pursuits of beach holidays, weekends away, camping and holiday camps. The Christmas section covers such familiarities as hectic preparations in the kitchen for family events, office parties, the Giles family Father bringing people back home for Christmas drinks at totally inconvenient times and Christmas shopping, while the Easter section sees a number of cartoons relating to weddings and flamboyant bonnets. As usual with Giles, the cartoons enclosed cover a wide range from events of national or international importance to more ordinary subjects such as the British weather. He would often contrive to link a number of these together in the same cartoon.

Recurring Themes

We find amongst the cartoons chosen, four recurring irritants which caused much annoyance to British holidaymakers and provided a fertile source of national grumbling: bad weather, traffic congestion, strikes and oil on the beach. This collection contains no fewer than 19 cartoons illustrating our famously unpredictable weather. Giles and his wife, Joan, took many holidays in this country and it is likely that their experiences of poor weather whilst away influenced his work. Giles, a keen "caravaner", designed and, I believe, built his own caravan in which a section of wall could be projected out from the main shell when stationary to accommodate a large drawing board. The photograph on page 160 clearly shows this feature in addition to the appalling weather conditions.

It is also likely that Giles and Joan experienced heavy traffic congestion en route around the country. This may well have prompted some of the cartoons of roads completely blocked with stationary vehicles, such as the one dated 2 August 1958 (page 22) in which even the well-marked alternative route is at a complete stand still. In addition, on 15 August 1961 (page 25), he aligned the Britons' annual summer rush to the beaches of the West Country with the construction of the Berlin Wall, which began two days earlier, causing many Germans to flee West.

Strikes were another blight on the British holiday season. The 29 July 1956 cartoon (page 19) shows strike action at a large car factory encroaching on the family seaside holiday, while that of 30 July 1972 (page 45) shows how a major dock strike can filter down and impact upon a small-scale river excursion.

Finally, the oil spillage problem, which spoilt many family holidays, features in a number of cartoons. On 27 May 1969 (page 37) Grandma used this as an excuse to be carried aloft in a beach chair-cum-chariot and on 27 May 1975 (page 49) the family dragged the mess back to their house after a bank holiday trip out.

Hidden Jokes

It is always worth looking carefully at the background of Giles's cartoons as they often contain other humorous details unrelated to the main theme, likely inserted for his own amusement. They include Stinker, the mop-haired boy from the family's neighbourhood, often with a camera capturing the family's antics – see the cartoon dated 28 July 1974 (page 47); Butch, the family dog with attitude, named after an American serviceman befriended by Giles and Joan during the war and seen in a cartoon from 17 December 1978 (page 111); and even, occasionally, himself, as seen on 27 December 1953 (page 79).

Another hidden joke contained in this collection is the parrot given to Grandma as a Christmas present by some of the children, which made its first appearance on 21 December 1980 (page 113). Having noticed its existence only recently, I have since discovered its presence in many more cartoons between 1980 and 1986, including eight in this collection. They show the parrot, usually up to no good, in the background of cartoons where Grandma, its mistress, is in the family home. We should have known that the parrot meant trouble from the beginning, with both the twins ending up injured on the first day of its arrival into the family. It is usually well hidden, and I am not certain that I have been able to list all of the cartoons in this collection where it makes an appearance (see page 114). Readers will have to look very closely to see it in the background.

Also, perhaps not everyone has noted that Giles's cartoons sometimes show a degree of animosity towards Rupert Bear, another character appearing in the *Express* newspapers. I suspect this is because Giles saw Rupert as a rival to his cartoon family for the affections of the newspapers' readers. Again, this hostility is only revealed after careful investigation of the background of some of the cartoons. In some, Rupert is seen hanging by the neck from a light fitting or being shot at by a posse of Giles family children. It is understood that attempts were made at the newspaper offices to remove these before they got into print but, inevitably, some slipped through. One such is in the cartoon from 24 December 1979 (page 112), where Rupert is being punched off a cupboard by Donald Duck.

It also pleased Giles occasionally to incorporate local Suffolk characters and friends in a cartoon. This included publicans, doctors and nurses, police, shop assistants and others. In the cartoon dated 19 August 1980 (page 61) we see Charlie Brinkley, a well-known ferryman and fisherman at Felixstowe Ferry in Suffolk, close to Giles's farm, and a good friend of the cartoonist. Giles, a keen yachtsman and, for many years, President of the Felixstowe Ferry Sailing Club, included Charlie in a number of his drawings.

The Latest Update on the Grandma Giles Sisterhood

As I worked on last year's collection I noted that, over the years, Giles's cartoons showed that Grandma had two sisters up north, another in Aberdeen, a fourth somewhere near Aberystwyth and yet another in Ireland – a total of five sisters excluding her. At the time, I warned readers that this may not be the final count.

As it turned out, prior to publication, I felt obliged to report that, unfortunately, another cartoon had emerged indicating that she had a further sister, Ivy, living somewhere near her, presumably in Suffolk. This made a total of seven of them, including Grandma, with perhaps one or more in Australia, resulting from her father's enforced stay in the Botany Bay Penal Colony for an unspecified crime. At the time, I had rather hoped that this was the total Grandma sisterhood.

However, in preparing this collection, I regret to report that another British sister, named Florrie, has turned up in the cartoon dated 19 August 1980 (page 61), marooned in France with Grandma sailing away to rescue her, much to Charlie Brinkley's bewilderment. I can no longer feel confident that this is the final list as further perusal of Giles's vast workload of cartoons may reveal others. We can only hope that this is not the case.

John Field

Summer Holidays

A replica Viking longship, called the "Hugin", had sailed across the North Sea from Denmark and arrived at Broadstairs in Kent.

The back seat boys.

Sunday Express, 31 July 1949

The Korean War began when North Korea invaded South Korea on 25 June 1950. Two days later President Truman ordered US air and sea forces to help the South Korean regime. On 4 July, the Soviet Deputy Foreign Minister accused the United States of starting armed intervention on behalf of South Korea. The next day, "Task Force Smith", comprising 400 US infantry, supported by an artillery battery, was moved to Osan, south of the South Korean capital Seoul, and ordered to fight as a rearguard.

"Repeat that last paragraph I read to you about the situation in Korea."

Daily Express, 11 July 1950

The holidaymaker is referring to the "Skylon" at the Festival of Britain in London – a futuristic-looking, slender, vertical, steel structure. Parliament discussed whether it constituted a danger to visitors by attracting lightning-strikes.

"Blackpool's got everything t' Festival's got, lad – except one o' those things where you get all struck by lightning if you're underneath."

Daily Express, 24 May 1951

"Mum! That man's thrown all our toffee and oranges out of the window."

Daily Express, 31 July 1951

After 14 months of preparation, the coronation of Queen Elizabeth II was due to take place, at Westminster Abbey, two weeks following the appearance of this cartoon. There was huge national interest in the event during this period and no doubt there was a very high level of security in place around the crown jewels – an essential part of this historic ceremony – so the joke was obviously not a good idea.

"They said, 'Anything on board there shouldn't be?' and for a joke I said, 'Only the Crown Jewels,' so for a joke they said, 'O.K. there's five minutes before your ship leaves – let's have her down to make sure.'"

Daily Express, 18 May 1953

This was the period when holiday camps were a very popular form of vacation in Britain. The camps were designed to encourage holidaymakers to stay on site and provided a wide range of entertainments as well as full eating facilities. However, I am not sure that Grandma is really enjoying her visit to the rather crowded swimming pool.

HOLIDAY CARTOON – Life in a Holiday Camp.

Sunday Express, 2 August 1953

Records show that the summer of 1954 was very poor with a great deal of rain, very cool temperatures and little sunshine.

"What d'you bet this one says – 'Cold for the time of year' or 'Dreadful weather for July'?"

Sunday Express, 11 July 1954

Giles, a fervent sailor himself, was commenting upon a national characteristic.

Determination of the British to ensure that their sons inherit our traditional love of the sea.

Daily Express, 2 August 1954

Since the spring, the British Government at the time was extremely concerned about the possibility of severe fuel shortages during the coming winter. Its fears were borne out with records showing that the winter of 1955 was the coldest and snowiest on record between the two "Big Freezes" of 1947 and 1963.

"That's a nice thing to say to Grandma when she asked you what our coal stock's like at home."

Sunday Express, 17 July 1955

Some workers at the British Motor Corporation Austin factory at Longbridge, in Birmingham, had been on strike. Two days earlier, the factory had closed down for the annual two-week holiday.

"My Harry's a striker on holiday – the other one's his boss who happens to be staying at our hotel."

Daily Express, 29 July 1956

The year 1957 saw many exhibitions and events relating to the fine arts taking place in the Union of Soviet Socialist Republics. They were aimed at promoting international recognition of their cultural importance and also at encouraging tourism.

"Certainly not, Edward. We might like it."

Daily Express, 28 May 1957

"There'll be some hollering when we get in – I locked Grandma in the bathroom before we went away."

Sunday Express, 11 August 1957

At this time, very high levels of traffic congestion regularly occurred at the beginning of August on the weekend prior to bank holiday Monday. Parliament began to debate a solution and finally, in 1965, the bank holiday in England, Wales and Northern Ireland was changed to the last Monday of August rather than the first. It remains the first Monday of the month in Scotland.

"Anybody seen one that matches this one? Escaped half an hour ago."

Daily Express, 2 August 1958

After a long period of beautiful summer weather, nearly 11millimetres (½ inch) of rain fell in London on 28 July and the maximum temperature the next day was only 17.7°C (63.9°F).

"Remember how we laughed at the Joneses for wasting their money going abroad with a lovely summer like this at home?"

Daily Express, 30 July 1959

Records show that the country experienced unsettled weather throughout July. Two days earlier, following a conference in London about possible independence, the government had decided to send a battalion of the Duke of Wellington's Regiment to Kenya, which, no doubt, was enjoying better weather.

"First time your father's smiled this holiday – when they told him he'd got to rejoin his regiment for Kenya."

Daily Express, 28 July 1960

Construction on the Berlin Wall commenced two days before this cartoon appeared. Its purpose was to prevent East Berliners and other Germans from crossing into the Western zones of the city. Its demolition, after a period of public unrest, began in June 1990. In the UK, this was another summer when the roads down to the West Country suffered considerable congestion.

"Another refugee trying to escape to the West."

Daily Express, 15 August 1961

Cowes Week, on the Isle of Wight, usually takes place in the first week of August. It is an eight-day sailing regatta and is one of the earliest sporting events in UK history, dating from 1826. It was originally known as the Royal Yacht Squadron Regatta which, perhaps, explains the name Giles gave to the large yacht.

"Sid, there's a bloke hollering something about we're on his mooring. What's a mooring, Sid?"

Sunday Express, 5 August 1962

British seaside landladies sometimes had a poor reputation which was not always deserved. The 1960s saw a big increase in British holidaymakers going abroad due to the attraction of packaged tours and the improved opportunities provided by cheaper flights. The records tell us that August that year was “cool with above average rainfall and below average sunshine”.

“Dad! Mum says come back and scratch out what you wrote in the Visitors’ Book at once.”

Sunday Express, 12 August 1962

Another reference to traffic congestion at holiday time.

"Don't say it! Don't you dare say you knew as soon as I'd got it up the traffic would move on."

Daily Express, 4 June 1963

The London weather report for that month stated, "A thundery breakdown late on the 2nd was followed by rain on the 3rd which amounted to nearly 12 millimetres (½ inch). During the remainder of the month there were very few days when the temperature exceeded 20°C (68°F), and it was generally rather cloudy with showers or longer spells of rain or drizzle".

"Having a wonderful time – three days in here to get out of the rain."

Daily Express, 6 August 1963

This cartoon would have referred to conditions two or three days before when the weather report stated, "over 30 millimetres (1¼ inches of rain fell with a high of only 16°C (60°F)". Presumably the action of the Pest Control Service was purely accidental.

"That's your father – always looking on the bright side – 'Do we realise that from today the nights start drawing in and we'll soon be thinking about Christmas cards."

Sunday Express, 21 June 1964

The weather report for mid-July 1964 stated, “After two or three showery days with broken sunshine, rain from another Atlantic depression reached western districts late on the 10th and spread to the remainder of the country during the night. A secondary depression gave over an inch of rain in parts of South Wales on the 11th and it was not until the afternoon of the 12th that the rain finally cleared southeast England”.

“Off they go – another load of little postcards saying we’re having a wonderful time and which won’t arrive until long after we’re home.”

Daily Express, 14 July 1964

"Tell Auntie our holiday is now assured to unfailing success. Dad's discovered the man in the next hut is a supporter of the Town team."

Daily Express, 17 August 1965

On 16 May 1966, the National Union of Seamen launched its first national strike since 1911. The strikers wanted to get higher wages and to reduce the working week from 56 to 40 hours. The impact of the strike was enormous, causing considerable disruption to the country's trading situation. The strike finally came to an end the day this cartoon appeared.

"As I was saying, Bertha – not all of 'em wanted to return to work."

Daily Express, 1 July 1966

Giles would not have been a great supporter of families crowding into public houses.

"Two iced lollies and a packet of bubbly gum ruddy well isn't what I ordered."

Sunday Express, 13 August 1967

"And this comment from your music teacher – 'I hope your boy enjoys his holiday as much as I'm going to enjoy mine'..."

Sunday Express, 21 July 1968

The final day of the 4th Ashes cricket match held at Leeds. The match was drawn meaning that Australia retained the Ashes. The wife's "announcement" almost certainly took place at a rather tense moment in this important match.

"We've got cousin Willy at silly mid-off, Auntie Ivy at deep fine leg, Uncle Harvey to bat, rain held off, so if our captain is ready to resume play…"

Daily Express, 30 July 1968

This was a period when oil spillage from vessels at sea was causing significant problems for holiday-makers on some British beaches.

"What's so special about Grandma's feet that she mustn't get oil on them like everybody else?"

Daily Express, 27 May 1969

"The young man says they're called purple hearts with LSD – they taste ever so nice."

Sunday Express, 31 August 1969

As the *Oriana* was leaving Southampton on 11 August a serious fire broke out in the boiler room. She had to return to her berth and the repairs took two weeks to complete.

"The owners have asked me to remind you, ladies and gentlemen, that this happens to be National Smile Week."

Daily Express, 13 August 1970

This is one of a few occasions when Giles includes himself in a cartoon – this time with a large glass of whisky, or something similar, in his hand.

Programme cover for 1970 International *Daily Express* Powerboat Race.

Daily Express, 22 August 1970

"Harry always takes an hour or so to make absolutely sure they're bathing in the nude before he reports them to the police."

Sunday Express, 25 July 1971

It would seem that this was another occasion when beaches were plagued with oil spillage from passing vessels.

"Our landlady on the Costa Brava last year didn't clap you in irons just because you've got oily feet."

Sunday Express, 1 August 1971

Cowes Week, on the Isle of Wight, is considered to be the largest sailing regatta of its kind in the world and was first held in 1826. “Britannia”, was the former royal yacht of Queen Elizabeth II and was in service from 1954 until 1997. It is estimated that during her career, she travelled more than a million nautical miles around the globe. Today, she is a visitor attraction berthed at Leith, Edinburgh.

“Ahoy there, dear – are you ready? The Britannia’s arrived – wind North to North-East – only light showers, lovely day for a spinnaker run.”

Daily Express, 3 August 1971

This refers to Sir Francis Chichester, a nationally-acclaimed English yachtsman who had undertaken a solo circumnavigation of the world in 1966–7. He was taken ill midway through a transatlantic race a few weeks before this cartoon and had to be assisted by the Royal Navy. Sadly, he died two months after the appearance of this cartoon.

"Why can't we have half the Navy come to our rescue like Sir Francis? Because we're not off the bloody mooring yet, that's why."

Sunday Express, 2 July 1972

A period when British ports were standing idle due to a dock workers' strike during which five "rebel" dock workers were jailed.

"Sorry about loading your own gear, chaps – got a spot of industrial dispute with me crew."

Sunday Express, 30 July 1972

"Not perhaps a bomb, but fairly large firework, maybe."

Sunday Express, 26 August 1973

1974 was not a good year for foreign holidays. Due to industrial unrest early in the year, a three-day working week was introduced and, consequently, holiday bookings dropped by 30 per cent. A number of tourist companies went bankrupt during the year and many thousands of holidaymakers faced major difficulties.

"As a matter of fact we do not think this is better than taking one of those chancy holidays in the Med."

Sunday Express, 28 July 1974

48 Following an early indication from the government that a general election was going to be called within a few weeks, newspapers reported that Jeremy Thorpe, the Liberal leader, had "jumped the gun" by storming West Country beaches in a hovercraft and "haranguing" holidaymakers.

"If it's not Jeremy Thorpe trying another stunt who is it?"

Sunday Express, 1 September 1974

This was a period of major problems with oil spillages from ships at sea on a number of the country's beaches.

"I'll tell you what I think about Bank Holidays by the sea."

Daily Express, 27 May 1975

“There goes Chalkie – off to the torrid beaches of St. Tropez for a rave-up on his newly gained riches.”

Daily Express, 25 July 1975

Earlier that week, a 3-tonne (3-ton) 9-metre (30-foot) bottlenose whale had become stranded on the beach near Clacton in Essex. Holidaymakers helped the authorities get the whale back into the water and it managed to swim safely out to sea.

"It keeps them amused – they read about those boys who revived a whale with pails of cold water."

Daily Express, 29 July 1975

General Francisco Franco ruled Spain from the end of the Spanish Civil War in 1939 until his death six weeks after this cartoon appeared. His period in power saw many accusations of political oppression in Spain and attracted much protest internationally. Four days earlier, all Spanish airline flights from Heathrow were "blacked" indefinitely by the unions, angered by the execution of five guerrillas by Spain's government.

"You didn't phone and cancel our Spanish holiday as a protest against Franco – you cancelled it because you damn well didn't want to go."

Sunday Express, 5 October 1975

"Do you think we could take one with a little more Olympic fire to show the Joneses when we get home?"

Daily Express, 9 February 1976

The Summer Olympics were being held in Montreal, Canada at this time.

"Thank goodness he didn't win – we'd never have got him up on the top one."

Sunday Express, 25 July 1976

The country was enjoying the hottest average summer temperature in the UK since records began. Unfortunately for the Giles family, however, severe thunderstorms at the end of August brought rain to some places for the first time in weeks including, obviously, where they had decided to holiday.

"Remember the hysterical laughter when I said 'Do we want to take our rain coats'?"

Sunday Express, 29 August 1976

"When I said build them a tree-house to keep them quiet, I didn't mean to include room service."

Sunday Express, 24 July 1977

"Here! Stick this Daily Express hat on – here comes my wife!"

Daily Express, 25 July 1978

58 Britain's airports were experiencing a period of chaos, with lengthy flight delays resulting from a "work to rule" protest by French air traffic controllers. It was reported that at Manchester Airport, performing dogs would be on hand to entertain holidaymakers plus a Punch and Judy show and cartoons and a Barbra Streisand film. Giles obviously decided to apply this approach to Heathrow.

"Can the Captain hang on till he sees who Mr Punch belts next – the parson or the copper?"

Sunday Express, 13 August 1978

Three days earlier, Brighton became the first major resort in Britain to officially provide part of its beach solely for nude bathers.

"Far enough, Adonis."

Sunday Express, 12 August 1979

"Hear that, everybody? If some of you don't start enjoying yourselves Father won't bring us again next year."

Sunday Express, 26 August 1979

The location is Felixstowe Ferry in Suffolk – a few miles from Giles's farm. Occasionally Giles would put someone he knew into a cartoon – in this case, the man with the bike is Charlie Brinkley, who was a well-known local character and a friend of the cartoonist. In this cartoon Giles was reminding readers that the 40th anniversary of the Dunkirk evacuation was a few weeks earlier. In the background, across the mouth of the River Deben, is one of the tall masts, now demolished, of the Bawdsey Manor Radar Station, which played an important role in defence during World War II.

"She says we made Dunkirk in 1940, so we can make it again to pick up her sister, Florrie"

Daily Express, 19 August 1980

This was a good year for British runner Sebastian Coe, having set world records in a number of track events.

"Thanks to your witty 'Here comes Sebastian Coe' he's now serving everybody else first."

Sunday Express, 30 August 1981

"Poor Penelope – she thought they were going back THIS Tuesday."

Daily Express, 1 September 1981

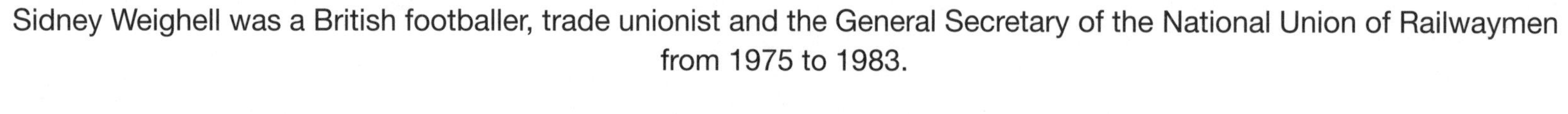

Sidney Weighell was a British footballer, trade unionist and the General Secretary of the National Union of Railwaymen from 1975 to 1983.

"He's been confined to the car for butting in with 'Sid Weighell's a goodun' [sic] when Auntie Bertha was running on about Union bosses."

Sunday Express, 18 July 1982

The Queen had had a difficult week but it was reported that she was "absolutely determined that everyone here should enjoy themselves" at the Buckingham Palace Garden Party being held that weekend, with 9,000 invited guests. Two days earlier, two bomb blasts by the IRA had occurred in central London – one blast blew up a bandstand in Regent's Park, killing a number of Royal Green Jackets bandsmen and wounding many in the audience and, on the same day, a car bomb in Hyde Park killed three soldiers and seven horses from the Queen's Life Guard.

"I appreciate the Queen has had more than her share for one week, but at least she hasn't got to put up with you lot on holiday for six-and-a-half."

Daily Express, 22 July 1982

That July was one of the hottest months on record with the temperature over 27°C (81°F) for 16 days. Reports stated that "the warmth caused asphalt roads to 'bleed' and stone dust had to be spread to prevent the road surface breaking up". The use of garden water hoses was banned. The month ended with heavy rain, thunder and lightning but obviously the authorities took a little while to catch up.

"You're still liable for prosecution, sir, the ban has not been officially lifted yet."

Daily Express, 2 August 1983

"Of course it's not a very good snap of you, Grandma – that's a snap of the old harbour buoy on the end of the pier."

Daily Express, 25 August 1983

Meteorologists tell us that, occasionally, Britain can experience storm-force winds and rain during the summer, which are often caused by a dying hurricane that has intensified on its journey across the Atlantic. This happened in August 1985 with strong winds and heavy rain across most of Britain.

"The Skipper's not coming – too wet. He's left the food on board and instructions if you'd like to take her on your own."

Sunday Express, 25 August 1985

"Stop calling him that every time we come past – it's not his fault your team lost their first game!"

Sunday Express, 24 August 1986

"They're paying in gold bullion for six vanilla cornets and they want £24,997.60 change."

Sunday Express, 10 July 1988

The government had just announced proposals to "crack down on litter louts". These proposals included a maximum fine increase from £400 to £1,000, with additional powers for local authorities to impose on-the-spot fines.

"Before we start the holidays we're all going to sign a little form declaring we all pay our own litter fines."

Sunday Express, 23 July 1989

Christmas

The government had just introduced the 1949 Patents Act with new provisions relating to imports and exports.

“You were then seen to enter yet another house where you did again wilfully distribute toys without import or export licence...”

Sunday Express, 25 December 1949

She may have found the roller skates interesting.

"Let's buy Grandma something really useful – like a train-set or some roller skates."

Daily Express, 12 December 1950

"God rest you merry, gentlemen, let nothing you dismay..."

Sunday Express, 14 December 1950

This was a period of severe coal shortages, both for industry and households.

"Dad – he's pinching our coal."

Daily Express, 24 December 1950

In November that year, British climber Eric Shipman had returned from an expedition on Mount Everest with photographs showing what could have been footprints of an Abominable Snowman. This set off considerable speculation about the possibility of such a creature existing.

"We've abominable robins, abominable Santa Clauses at abominable prices – but no snowmen."

Daily Express,13 December 1951

At this time Parliament was discussing shop closing hours. The average working hours, for all workers, was estimated to be around 48 hours a week, with shop-workers often working into the early evening.

Despondency among the little ones overhearing Father Christmas discussing in very unseasonable terms the suggestion that shopworkers should work longer hours.

Sunday Express, 30 November 1952

Giles had spent Christmas recovering from (according to him) pneumonia. Several cartoons appeared at this time informing the world of this fact and obviously the Giles family children were expecting the worst. Their plans were thwarted when he appeared at the gate.

"Stop making holly wreaths, everybody – he's up."

Sunday Express, 28 December 1952

I am not convinced that they are going to get away with it. Is that Giles sitting next to Grandma?

"Now for peace sake – don't tell the Missus we've had a drink."

Sunday Express, 27 December 1953

Giles did spend various periods in Ipswich Hospital and sometimes he would include in his hospital cartoons doctors and nurses who had had the misfortune of having to deal with him. It is almost certain that the doctor shown here was one such unfortunate.

Dedicated to all those compelled to spend Christmas in hospital, where there is little or no escape from giving a hand with the decorations. I know, I've had some.

Daily Express, 24 December 1954

At this time, many thousands of US service personnel were stationed in the UK, including the area around Giles's part of the country, and some were fortunate enough to be invited into British homes for Christmas day.

"Top sergeant says to pass word round that if someone don't start getting festive pretty soon he's gonna bust the lot of us in the morning."

Sunday Express, 26 December 1954

Another Christmas hospital scene – again the two doctors (bottom left-hand and right-hand corners) were almost certainly known to Giles as they both appear in a number of his other hospital and medical cartoons.

Once again we dedicate our Christmas cartoon to all those spending the holiday in hospital; safe and sound from the Yuletide hullabaloo going on outside.

Daily Express, 24 December 1955

"His Royal Highness – King of the Office Parties – home bang on time as usual to help with the decorations."

Sunday Express, 23 December 1956

"They've got a point there, Taffy – Christmas Eve is a nice time to come home and say we've forgotten the turkey."

Daily Express, 24 December 1957

"Sorry, folks, we can't show you our holiday films and baby's first birthday party – projector's packed up."

Sunday Express, 21 December 1958

"I suppose you remember on Christmas Eve inviting the office staff to celebrate the Paper's 40th Birthday this evening?"

Sunday Express, 28 December 1958

"When you flicked the Boss one across the ear with that sprig of holly and said 'Merry Christmas' I didn't think much of the way he said 'And a prosperous New Year to you.'"

Daily Express, 22 December 1959

"Miss! That was not the way to reply to Modom's request for a suggestion what to send her sister Millie."

Daily Express, 14 December 1961

In December 1962 the British submarine-based Polaris weapons system programme was announced following an agreement between the US and UK governments. Giles is suggesting that this decision had a major impact upon the British children's fireworks market.

"Here comes another one – 'My-boy-says-Skybolts-are-out-of-date-can-he-change-it-for-a-Polaris?'"

Daily Express, 13 December 1962

"How about that? Chalkie buying scent and we haven't got a camera."

Daily Express, 22 December 1962

This was the first Christmas after the passing of the Road Traffic Act, 1962 which explored the possibility of using blood, urine or breath for alcohol analysis in considering a person's "ability to drive properly". In fact, no actual legal drink-driving limit was introduced until five years later.

"I thought you said there would be only soft drinks at the office party."

Daily Express, 24 December 1962

Another hospital scene. The doctor who appears in the cartoon dated 24 December 1955 (see page 82), also appears here and the nursing sister in front of him, sitting at the desk, is based on the sister in Giles's ward at Ipswich Hospital who, it was said, was the only one who could keep him under control. She appears in a number of his cartoons featuring hospital scenes.

"If you're fit enough to do the decorating around here you're fit enough to come home and do ours."

Daily Express, 17 December 1963

"Hang on a minute – I'm sure George would love to come over to tea and see the new baby..."

Sunday Express, 27 December 1964

"Never mind who hit who first – put the boy down."

Daily Express, 14 December 1965

"Hi, George! We've just popped in for a quick one with your wife before Christmas – like you asked us at the party last night."

Daily Express, 22 December 1966

96 With growing racial tension in the country, the South African government passed a Terrorism Act in June 1967 and, in September, military service became compulsory for all white men in South Africa over the age of 16. Earlier, in October 1964, after considerable pressure from the Anti-Apartheid Movement in Britain, the Prime Minister, Harold Wilson, instructed the Board of Trade in London to stop arms exports to South Africa although existing contracts were to be honoured. This was followed by a period of dissent in Britain against the trading ban but, the day before this cartoon appeared, Wilson informed Parliament that the arms ban would remain.

"Mum, can our Arms to South Africa debating group use the front room on Christmas Eve?"

Daily Express, 19 December 1967

Apollo 8 was launched by the US on 21 December 1968 and became the first manned spacecraft to leave the Earth's orbit and to reach the Moon, orbit it and return safely to Earth. The astronaut crew of three were Commander Frank Borman, Command Module Pilot James Lovell and Lunar Module Pilot William Anders. Giles may have been expressing his own views regarding the excesses of the festive season.

"Know who I vote the Three Wise men this Christmas? Those three who've hoofed it round the other side of the moon."

Sunday Express, 22 December 1968

"For an archdeacon's daughter working part time, that wasn't a bad mouthful."

Daily Express, 16 December 1969

"Go tell Father Christmas that Mummy Christmas has come to join the office party."

Daily Express, 22 December 1970

"Tonight at 21.00 hours precisely there will be a 15-minute truce while Auntie Lily sings 'The Indian Love Call'."

Daily Express, 28 December 1971

"The purpose of this sale is to dispose of our own surplus junk, madam, not to acquire yours."

Daily Express, 28 December 1972

"You lot aren't here to bring me comfort and joy – you're here to save your blooming light and heating at home."

Sunday Express, 23 December 1973

Two days earlier, petrol supply companies had increased the wholesale price of petrol. This was a period of fuel shortages and, to add to the motorist's frustration, the government announced, four days earlier, that "British drivers must adhere to reduced speed limits from midnight tonight as the government tries to save fuel".

"Don't you Merry Christmas me at 73p a gallon!"

Daily Express, 19 December 1974

"'George', I said, 'Christmas Eve. What better time to ask our new neighbours round for a drink and meet Mummy'."

Daily Express, 24 December 1974

"O.K., Harodges, one Mother Christmas coming up – 36-24-38."

Daily Express, 18 December 1975

The Sex Discrimination Act was on its way.

"They're voting what to call Grandma after the Sex Discrimination Act begins tomorrow – 'Jaws' or 'Sir'."

Sunday Express, 28 December 1975

"On the Twelfth Day of Christmas my true love sent to me: A bill for the tu-ur-key, another for the whi-is-ky, and one for the little fir tree."

Daily Express, 6 January 1976

"I don't know who it is – we thought it was you."

Daily Express, 24 December 1976

"Good morning, Dad. The aunts say as you've got ten days off for Christmas they can stay another week."

Daily Express, 28 December 1976

This does not bode well for the success of the forthcoming office party.

"You can get that damn thing off my desk for a start!"

Daily Express, 19 December 1977

I am not sure that Butch the dog agrees with the vote.

"Right – on the show of hands Sebastian gets a reprieve – one of you go to the shop and get six large tins of corned beef."

Sunday Express, 17 December 1978

"Dad, Mum says would you like a mince pie while we're waiting for the fire brigade?"

Daily Express, 24 December 1979

"You've bought Grandma a WHAT for Christmas?"

Sunday Express, 21 December 1980

Grandma seems delighted with her present – perhaps she sees it as an accomplice in her attempts to cause chaos and confusion in the family's life. It would appear that the parrot survived at least six years – see the cartoons on pages 115, 118, 119, 120 (I think that is it at the top of the Christmas tree), 121 and 156.

"'Soon as the shops open after Christmas back goes the damn parrot.' 'Not so,' says the parrot."

Sunday Express, 28 December 1980

"Rejoice good Christian men – the group's arrived."

Daily Express, 24 December 1981

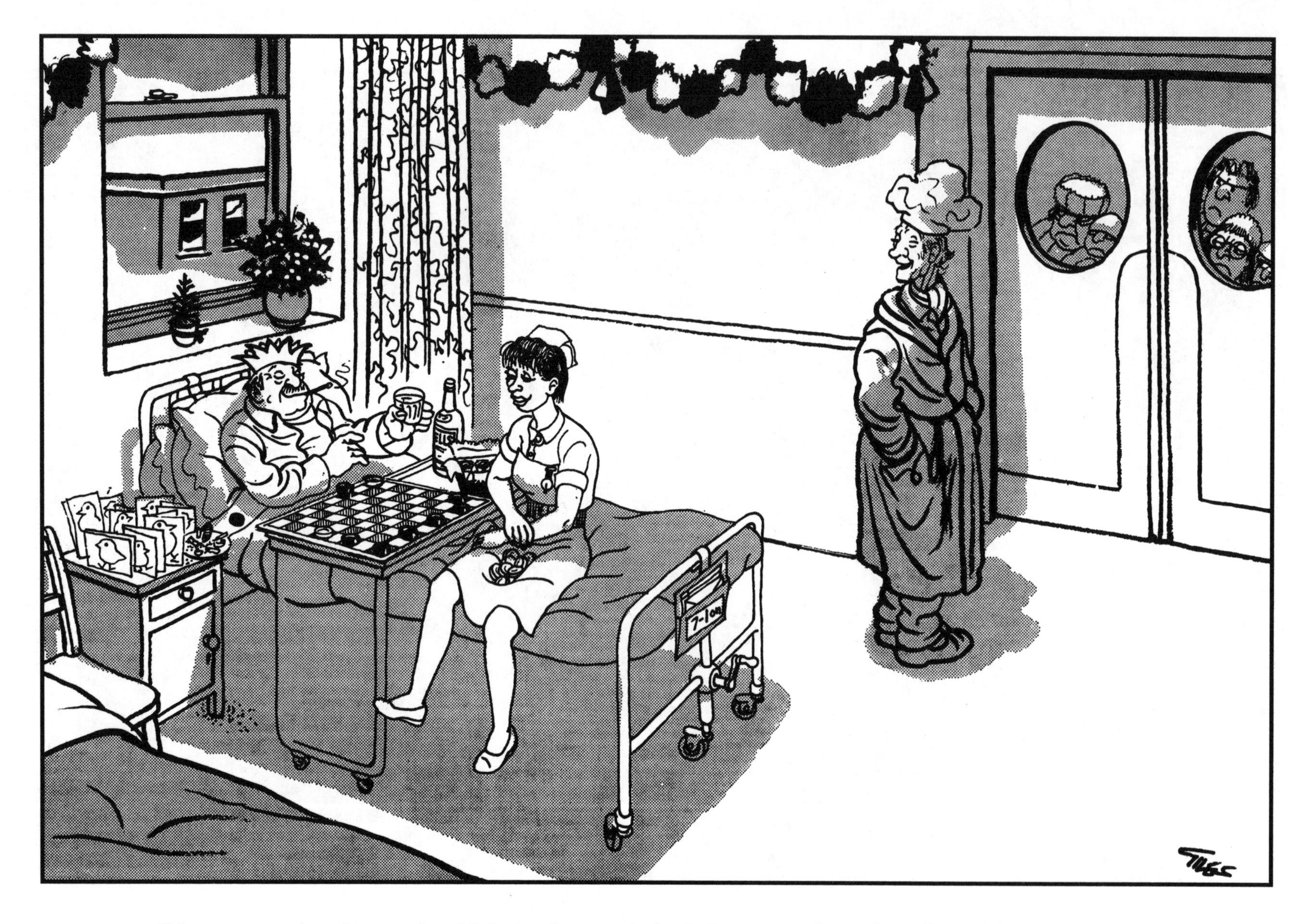

"You were saying, Harry, about it being heaven to be in here away from the wife and family for a bit."

Sunday Express, 27 December 1981

Nurses at the time were complaining about Victorian-style working conditions, pay and staffing levels – without success.

"You want to watch the jokes – it's going to take them a little time to settle down after losing their claim."

Sunday Express, 19 December 1982

"It's the plumber we ordered in August – he can come and do the drain this afternoon."

Daily Express, 24 December 1982

"I don't know who he is – he called and said 'I'm Father Christmas' and he's been here all afternoon."

Daily Express, 24 December 1983

"That's the holly and the mistletoe – now all we want is an almighty bang when dad blows the fuses, then we know it's Christmas."

Sunday Express, 16 December 1984

"Noel! I've just won a Christmas holiday for one in the Bahamas – plane leaves tonight!"

Daily Express, 20 December 1984

"I know they haven't got a sale on – that's one of my boy's Christmas presents going back the moment they open."

Daily Express, 27 December 1984

Two days earlier, the world's first all-teddy-bear auction had taken place at Christie's, where 186 bears went under the hammer. The highest price achieved was £700 for a plush-covered 1910 bear. Grandma looks more guilty than normal – or is it the pianists?

"Those Teddy bears you 'found' up here and put in Christie's sale were the twins' Christmas presents."

Sunday Express, 15 December 1985

"He's never nipped anyone before – he probably thought you were going to mug him."

Daily Express, 24 December 1985

The Nimrod was a Hawker Siddeley maritime patrol aircraft. AWACS stood for Airborne Warning and Control System, which along with the Early Warning System were all part of the country's defence and preparation against a possible major conflict. MI5 is the Military Intelligence, Section 5 – relating to spies; EEC was the European Economic Community, which lasted from 1957 until 1993 when it was incorporated into the European Community (EC); and the AIDs epidemic, at this time, was spreading around the world. Not the best set of subjects at a festive season office party.

"In the right corner – Nimrod, AWACS, early warning systems. In the left corner – MI5, EEC and AIDs etc."

Daily Express, 18 December 1986

"Dad says the Germans have got it right banning Forces Christmas parties in Germany – he says he's for banning Christmas parties everywhere."

Daily Express, 20 December 1988

"Oh dear, they all left an hour ago – they thought they were staying with you for Christmas."

Daily Express, 24 December 1989

Easter

"As usual we all made plans for Easter. And as usual only Mother's came to anything."

Daily Express, 16 April 1949

Obviously an atypically British Easter in terms of weather.

Determination of the British to have their weddings at Easter.

Daily Express, 12 April 1952

This cartoon appeared during the tense period building up to the Vietnam War. With the military defeat of the French earlier in the year, a 1954 Geneva meeting partitioned Vietnam into North and South, and the French withdrew from Vietnam. This period saw increasing US involvement in the area and judging from what appears to be a heavy gun barrel in the background, this factory was involved in the armaments business. Giles was probably suggesting that the management was anticipating heavy demand for its products requiring overtime working.

"Sorry, chum – overtime. Friday, Saturday, Sunday, Monday."

Daily Express, 15 April 1954

Giles was making a comment about something which obviously annoyed him as a rural dweller.

"Hey – you missed one."

Sunday Express, 1 April 1956

Easter is, of course, a popular period for marriages and an excuse for elaborate and extraordinary hats.

"When I said 'For better or worse' yesterday I hadn't seen that hat."

Sunday Express, 21 April 1957

There was considerable debate in Parliament about whether throwing confetti at a wedding was an offence under the Litter Bill, which was being discussed at that time.

"Here we are, litter bugs."

Sunday Express, 6 April 1958

It is recorded that around this time westerns were an audience favourite on TV and 1959 was the peak year for such programmes.

“Dear Maud, we are staying at a very nice hotel right on the sea front. The weather is lovely and it is such a change to get away from the house for a few days…”

Sunday Express, 29 March 1959

"Sidney – did you put a bee in Miss Emily's Easter bonnet?"

Sunday Express, 17 April 1960

"If you mutter 'Do you mean to say that cost four pounds nineteen and eleven?' once more, I'm going home."

Sunday Express, 2 April 1961

Grandma is not really embracing the spirit of the period of "Peace on Earth and Goodwill to All Men"!

"I suppose you will be spending three days of this joyous holiday beseeching that a pestilence fall upon the visiting team and the ref. be maimed."

Daily Express, 19 April 1962

"Listening to everybody repeating 'And to think we're paying over twenty pounds for a weekend of it' is getting on Captain's nerves."

Sunday Express, 29 March 1964

"I trust I shall see something of you during the Easter Holiday?"

Daily Express, 15 April 1965

Over the Easter period, some parts of the country experienced very cold weather and snow showers.

"Daddy and I think it might all have been more worthwhile had you come somewhere in the first twenty of the Easter Parade Beauty competition."

Daily Express, 20 April 1965

On 19 February 1967, the supertanker SS *Torrey Canyon* left Kuwait with a full cargo of crude oil. She struck a reef off Cornwall on 18 March and caused one of the world's worst oil spills. Hundreds of miles of coastline in Britain, France, Guernsey and Spain were affected.

"To think we didn't go to the seaside because of oil on the beaches."

Sunday Express, 26 March 1967

This was a period of peace marches, particularly against the war in Vietnam.

"If you really cared about peace you wouldn't have overslept so we missed the other marchers."

Sunday Express, 14 April 1968

"O.K. Barker, we've got the message – you had a heatwave in Southend-on-Sea and we all had it belting with rain in Majorca."

Daily Express, 8 April 1969

Part of Giles's long-standing "war" with traffic wardens – another poor Easter in terms of weather.

"Achtung! A car!"

Daily Express, 31 March 1970

As Giles noted, Princess Anne, at the time, "had made some caustic comments on the new hot pants fashion".

"May I have a show of hands for all those in favour of Princess Anne's comments on hot pants."

Sunday Express, 11 April 1971

The exhibition was opened by the Queen three days before this cartoon appeared and, although planned to run for six months, it was so popular that it was extended until 30 December. It was estimated that almost 1,700,000 visitors saw the exhibition. The policeman seems to be enjoying his job.

"Pardon me, Tutankhamun, but your tootsies are parked on the double yellow lines."

Sunday Express, 2 April 1972

Easter is always a busy period for weddings.

"I knew that registrar would bungle two dozen Easter weddings at the same time – here comes your bridegroom now."

Sunday Express, 22 April 1973

Poor weather over Easter again!

"Nothing's going to stop him giving the lawn its Easter hair cut with his new mower."

Sunday Express, 30 March 1975

A week earlier the government announced that tax on fuel would be increased by 7.5p a gallon.

"We're not at the mercy of airline strikes – not using petrol at 79p a gallon – think of the rail and bus fares we're saving and will I stand up straight and look as if we're enjoying it."

Sunday Express, 18 April 1976

"'Let's spend Easter in that same little hotel we spent our honeymoon?' Me too."

Sunday Express, 26 March 1978

This was a period of rapidly increasing air travel and the media were reporting that long delays could be expected as the country's existing airport provision was proving to be inadequate.

"Bill's got us a honeymoon suite in a nice quiet shady nook out of the draught at London Airport."

Daily Express, 12 April 1979

"Finish making Grandma's Easter egg later and tell her breakfast is ready."

Sunday Express, 6 April 1980

"Julie – you know your Easter bonnet –"

Sunday Express, 19 April 1981

 The ten-week Falklands War between Argentina and the UK started on 2 April, and both sides were keen to acquire more ships to help their war efforts.

"You'll have to make your mind up quick, sir – I've had an offer from the Government and the Argentinians."

Sunday Express, 11 April 1982

The debate about the rights and wrongs of fox hunting was in full swing at this time.

"Any political party who ban horses as well as fox hunting will get my vote."

Sunday Express, 3 April 1983

 The country experienced stormy weather towards the end of March causing damage including trees being blown over.

"Shame they can't move that fallen tree in front of the garden tool shed until after Easter."

Sunday Express, 30 March 1986

The bad weather continued.

"Good morning, girls – I trust your holiday has invigorated you and you're looking forward to the Spring Sales."

Daily Express, 1 April 1986

The 1987 World Snooker Championship took place at the Crucible Theatre in Sheffield and started the day before this cartoon appeared.

"Trafford – kindly tell that Guide my private TV quarters are strictly out of bounds to tourists."

Sunday Express, 19 April 1987

"This isn't Dad – it's a straw-packed dummy!"

Sunday Express, 26 March 1989

Carl Giles had been cartoonist for Lord Beaverbrook's *Daily* and *Sunday Express* for almost 20 years, when on 20 March 1962 the Conservative MP Sir Martin Lindsay tabled a motion deploring "the conduct of Lord Beaverbrook in authorizing over the last few years in the newspapers controlled by him more than 70 adverse comments on members of the royal family who have no means of replying".

Lindsay was wrong about the royal family having no means of reply. That day Prince Philip also vented his anger at Beaverbrook's campaign, during a press reception at the British Embassy in Rio de Janeiro. According to the paper's Brazil representative, the Prince declared that„ "The *Daily Express* is a bloody awful newspaper. It is full of lies, scandal and imagination. It is a vicious paper."

When the *Daily Express* reported this the next day, Giles decided to treat it as a joke. He knew the royal family enjoyed his cartoons; they often asked for the artwork. This had begun in 1948, when Prince Philip was sent a cartoon on the State Opening of Parliament, and over the next few years Giles received a steady stream of requests from Buckingham Palace for original drawings.

Giles drew the diminutive Lord Beaverbrook being escorted through the Traitor's Gate at the Tower of London, with a headsman's axe and block standing ready in the background. The caption repeated Prince Philip's condemnation of the *Daily Express*, but added laconically: "'Ah well,' said Lord B., as they trotted him off to the Tower, 'at least he takes it or he wouldn't know it was a bloody awful newspaper.'"

This was a brilliant response, which did much to defuse the situation. When Giles's cartoon was printed the next day, *Daily Express* staff were surprised to receive a phone call from the Queen's press secretary, with a message for Giles that "Her Majesty requests today's cartoon to commemorate one of her husband's most glorious indiscretions."

Giles sent off the artwork and in May 1962 found himself invited to "a small informal luncheon party" at Buckingham Palace with the Queen and Prince Philip. "I was filled with absolute dread," Giles recalled afterwards. "But as soon as she started to talk I was put at my ease...There were about half a dozen corgis running about in a completely uncontrolled state. Suddenly the Queen shouted, 'HEP'. It was like a bark from a sergeant major. The corgis immediately stood to attention. Then filed out of the room."

Right: Giles and his wife Joan enjoying the British weather in Derbyshire in 1936.

After the lunch Giles mischievously drew a cartoon of the guests leaving with corgi-savaged trousers. He sent it to the Queen, who returned her thanks through one of her private secretaries, noting that she was "glad that you got away without having lost, at least to the best of her knowledge, so much as a shred of your trousers".

After that Giles became what one *Daily Express* journalist called "a kind of cartooning jester to the royal family". By the time he retired in 1991 the royal family had more than 40 of his original drawings, the largest number being owned by Prince Philip, who shared Giles's anarchic view of the world.

The British Cartoon Archive, based at the University of Kent's Templeman Library in Canterbury, is dedicated to the history of British cartooning over the last two hundred years. It holds the artwork for more than 150,000 British political and social-comment cartoons, plus large collections of comic strips, newspaper cuttings, books and magazines. Its website at www.cartoons.ac.uk has 200,000 cartoon images, including the majority of Carl Giles's published work.